Luang Prabang
watercolours & inks

by Somboon Phoungdorkmai

text of the author
with andré lurde & susan atkinson

Asia Horizons Books

Entrance of Tam Ting, a holy cave near Luang Prabang, reputed to shelter thousand of Buddha relics.

FOREWORD

This unique book is a result of the superb work of Thai artist Somboon Phoungdorkmai. From mid-1997, with a grant from the Thai-Lao Association she set up her easel in the Heritage City of Luang Prabang and for almost two years immersed herself in the daily life of its people.

Trips were organized at different seasons to capture the essence of life there. Being a Thai artist enabled Somboon to communicate in almost the same language as the people of Luang Prabang. This proved extremely useful in her exchanges and understanding of the locals who were frequently delighted with her presence.

Somboon also captures the mood of the many Buddhist inspired festivals held in the former capital, and especially the elaborate New Year Festival when people can view the Prabang, the most important Buddha image of the city. The book recounts the history of the places together with the experiences of the artist during her many months at work.

Luang Prabang watercolours

CONTENTS

A city of World Heritage

Treasure of Lan Chang

The aeroplane sank into the deep mattress of clouds. As it dipped some hundred yards lower, my nose pressed against the window, I caught a glimpse of the Wat Phousi temple's golden spire perched on top of the small hill, which overlooks the city nestling between the legendary Mekong and Khan rivers. We landed somewhere in the outskirts of the town on the single run-away along which we had to walk to reach the airport building. A huge portfolio and a pad of water-colour paper more than one meter wide must have made me seem a strange tourist as, together with my husband and a group of backpackers, I jumped into the back of the tuk -tuk which was to take us to where we would be staying. On the way, on the lower slopes of the hills to our left, rays of sunlight were reflected on a golden pagoda during the late afternoon light. Built some fif-teen years before, the Santi Chedi is the most recent religious building and forms part of thirty or so other valued Bhuddist temples that make up the treasure of Luang Prabang.

My first ink study achieved was about Wat Sen.

A number of legends surround the birth of the town during the 16th or 17th Century. According to one tale, the Mount Phousi, shaped like a heap of rice, was chosen by two hermits as the place to settle down the town, foreseeing a wealthy future assured by the presence of this fertility symbol. Another story tells of how a smile would appear on the face of Lord Buddha when looking in the direction of this mount, surrounded as it is by two rivers. Intrigued by this, his cousin and disciple, Ananda, was told that a rich and powerful city would emerge from this location. As far as Laotians are concerned, the truth of these stories does not matter at all. They simply form part of the fabric of the town's rich history, which the present inhabitants use to maintain the continuation of traditional customs.

Originally named Muang Sua, then Xieng Dong Xieng Thong, the town gets its present name - Luang Prabang - from the time of the reign of King Fa Ngum (1316-1374) at the same time becoming the capital of Lane Xang, the Kingdom of a Million Elephants. The latter title comes from the Buddha Phra Bang, a gold-based alloy

In memory of the exhibition at Rajanakarn building where the full record of Somboon's paintings have been held.

That Chomsi golden spire on top of Phousi Mountain.

statue cast in Ceylon in the ninth century and then offered by the Khmer king, Paramantha Khemmaraja, to Prince Fa Ngum, his son-in-law, in 1358. At the end of the seventeenth century the kingdom was weakened by being broken up into several divisions and thus became successively preyed upon by the Burmese and Siamese. One of the greatest times of hardship, destruction and pillage occurred in 1887, organised by Deo Van Tri (Kham Oun in Laotian), commander of the Black Banners, Tai Khao armed gangs from Vietnam. France, through the intervention of Auguste Pavie, an explorer and diplomat, brought aid and protection during this troubled period. A special agreement with the King allowed the establishment of a colonial protectorate of Luang Prabang which ensured relative peace and stability until the fall of Indochina in 1954. Later this special place had a narrow escape from the horrors of the Vietnam War taking place on her very doorstep in the '70s, before the final collapse of the monarchy and the disappearance of the last king, Savang Vatthana. Eventually the communist government of the Lao Popular Democratic Republic was established in 1975.

This historical richness made the province a crossroads of cultures, and so it remains to this day. This heritage should not be overshadowed or forgotten. As soon as the Laotians authorities reopened the frontiers in 1992, UNESCO gave immediate recognition to the uniqueness of Luang Prabang by including the town in the list of the World Heritage sites in December 1995. Then at the beginning of 1997, just three months after my first visit, an official ceremony was arranged to pay respect to and consecrate Laotian tradition. As a witness to this event I felt I had to immortalise the moment by painting a picture of the Grand Palace at night, decorated with a large inaugural banner displayed on the front gate. I felt extremely proud and privileged to have the opportunity to act as reporter and record what I deemed to be an historic moment.

A friend, Khun Pissanu Chanvithan, a diplomat from the Thai Ministry of Foreign Affairs, was originally responsible for my presence in Laos during these celebrations. After hearing about a book I had published in 1996, made up partly of my drawings and water-colours of the temples of Angkor, he set about arranging a similar project to cover the town of Luang Prabang. Through the help of the Thai-Lao Association under the presidency of Khun Arsa Sarasin, he raised sufficient funds to allow me to spend several short stays there. It was agreed that the work I produced from this project would initially be shown during a public exhibition,

The metallic bridge over the Nam Khan river, unavoidable passage to reach the heart of town from the airport.

Joyful animation with the Hmong's ethnic group during their New Year festivities.

which was put on to strengthen the ties between Laos and Thailand. How delighted I was when I learned that Her Royal Highness, the Princess Maha Chakri Sirindhorn, was to do me the honour of opening the exhibition in August 1998 held in the Rajanakarn building on Sathorn Avenue in Bangkok, demonstrating yet again the great attachment which the Princess feels for Laos.

I must confess that my agreement to this venture was not instantaneous, as I was not sure of finding similar inspiration to that which had enabled me to be so productive during my earlier experience in the temples of Angkor. I had doubts about my ability to be able to immerse myself in this new subject with all the passion and concentration necessary to produce work of a quality that would be at least an equivalent. It was by describing to me the special qualities of Luang Prabang, which had preserved in many ways the feel of a village, that Khun Pissanu found the words that finally convinced me to accept the project. He drew a touching comparison between the peaceful atmosphere and timelessness that surrounded the town where he loves to go whenever he has the time, and his own gentle childhood in Thailand.

Even so my worries about finding something to inspire me was still with me as we crossed the metal bridge above the River Khan to reach the heart of this settlement. The sounds of the wooden struts crashing and knocking together kept time with the backfiring of the exhaust of the tuk-tuk and seemed to bid us welcome. The clouds of dust caused by the vehicles mixed with a light acrid smell of smoke irritated the eyes and caused some of the travellers to cough as we crossed the intersection in front of the covered market of the town centre. Among the small crowd some Hmong people, dressed in black costumes decorated with blue and multi-coloured embroidery, bustled about both in normal and the distinctive sidecar samlor taxis of Lang Prabang. It was the time of day when the supplies that had been bought with the daily income earned from the sale of handicrafts or wood or crops were being taken home.

Despite there being so much traffic here, there was no comparison with the pollution found in a capital city such as Bangkok, which I had left that morning. In fact, the smoke came mainly from wood fires lit by the housewives to prepare the evening meal in their backyards. A number of houses were not then equipped with gas or electric cookers, or even, in some cases, sanitary facilities. Among the buildings in a better state of repair and available to visitors we found one with a large guest-room and a balcony looking out on to the Mekong river. We returned to this same place every trip and it proved to be perfect for my work on rainy days. Moreover, I shall never forget the kindness nor the constant care and attention of the proprietors.

My initiation into the life of Luang Prabang started on my first morning as I witnessed the Tak Bat ceremony, when a procession of monks collect alms whilst sounding the reveille to wake up the town. In every part of town the inhabitants, wearing their traditional scarves, kneel on the pavements to greet the line of monks in their saffron and orange robes, flamboyant in the pale dawn. Following one of these groups going slowly and silently back up the main street, I caught the first flavours of what this town offered me with its rows of white or blue ochre walls and sombre wooden buildings, enriched at regular intervals by temples decorated in red and gold.

The Tak Bak: an every morning ritual of monks collecting alms.

As I passed in front of the steps that climb up to Mount Phousi, the original centre of the town, frangipani flowers were strewn about giving off their heady perfume, forever associated for me with Buddhist rituals. During Buddhist ceremonies the petals of these flowers are mixed with water, which is then sprayed over statues of Buddha, as well as the monks and their disciples. This first outing already gave me plenty of subject matter to paint and it seemed it would be possible, with patience and concentration, to produce interesting work.

The outlook and attitudes of the monks from these parts would become a vast source of information for my work and therefore me. Eventually, with me still following, the monks returned to their temple. After a short stop in the Wat Sen enclosure, in awe at the sight of the six columns of the magnificent and ornate façade, I followed a path through an alleyway thus leaving the back courtyard and came out onto an adjoining street. In front of their doorsteps several old people were already sitting on benches or stools, or even on the bare ground on straw

mats. Smiling, they shouted out to some school children, who were not in a hurry to get to school and were more inclined to dawdle on the way. Some of them, in-groups of three or four, had improvised a game consisting of throwing one of their sandals into a pile of scrap paper some ten yards in front of them. The winner would be the one who scattering the most paper thus gained the prize money, a pittance considering the amount of effort involved. It would nevertheless be enough to get extra sweets for them to chew.

Threading my way past these lively activities, I reached the road that runs alongside the banks of the Mekong. By this time it was mid morning and time for me to sit down at a table on the terrace of a local restaurant for a breakfast of noodle soup. The squeals of small black pigs being brought ashore drew my attention to the river activities. A number of different coloured boats came alongside loaded with passengers and merchandise. Whilst slowly swallowing the piping hot contents of my bowl, I delighted at the sights of a fisherman throwing his net from his boat out into mid-stream.

Or my eyes following the smoke escaping from a large cooking pot in front of the door of a bamboo cabin erected in the sand of the bank and a woman preparing a meal, whilst at the same time keeping an eye on a flock of young goats tied up to a post. Even the intermittent chugging of a slow-boat did not interrupt the serenity of the scene. On the contrary, it accentuated the rhythm of everyday life thereabouts.

The book you are now skimming through is a record of the pen sketches and water-colours that I completed over several months. With Luang Prabang citizens of all ages often at my side peeking over my easel, I was frequently working under critical eyes. Despite the excitement and the pleasure that all these spectacles brought me, worries concerning my work stayed with me. There was no lack of subjects for my paintings.

But there was still the question of how to capture the harmony of the country. In this book I hope that by relating anecdotes of my experiences, allied to explanations of my inspiration and examples of my work I will get you to share in my journey of discovery and that you too will feel the urge to visit or revisit Luang Prabang yourself one day.

The bank of the Mekong, giving its pace to the town.

The Great Palace adorned with the inaugural banner of UNESCO, appointing Luang Prabang as a city of the world heritage at the beginning of the Year 1998.

ຫລວງພະບາງ ເມືອງມໍລະດົກໂລກ
ຍິນດີຕ້ອນຮັບ

Preceeding double-page: Wat Sen, one other of the thirty or so temples that compose the treasure of Luang Prabang

At night, the Phousi Mountain stands as a protector of the town.

Still life with a natural composition of orchids from the luxuriant greenery that flourish on the front of the house of my welcoming family.

The venerated statue of the Buddha Phra Bang, the emblem of the town.

A bed of falling Champas, the flowers used to perfume water during Buddhist rituals.

A local production of fresh vegetables, grown on the banks of the Mekong.

The footsteps of Phousi Mountain under the spell of frangipani trees.

The Great Palace, residence of the last king of Laos, is nowadays a museum opened to visitors.

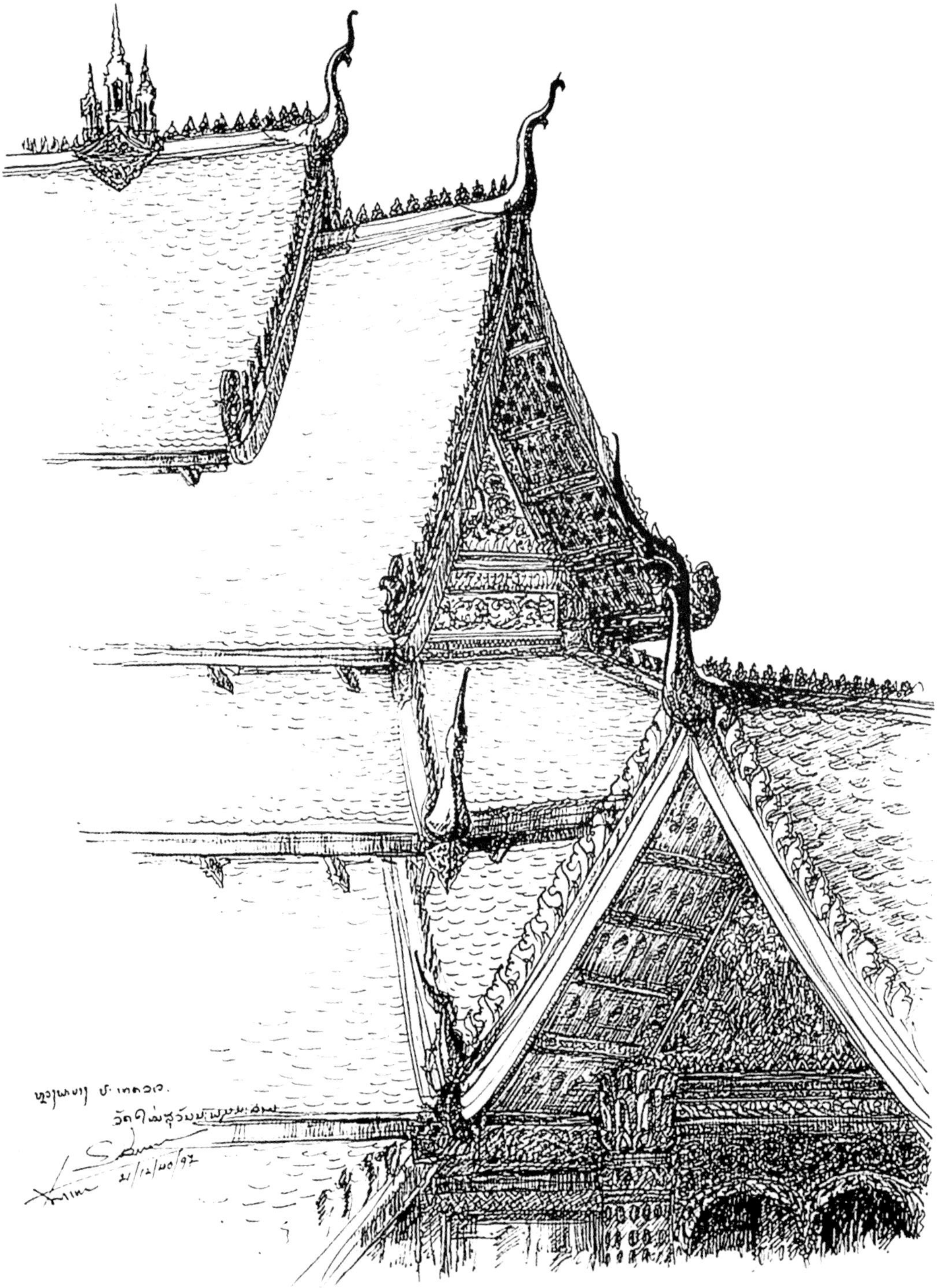

The very specific five-tiered roof on Wat Mai.

The city of Buddha

Pagodas in the landscape

At the start of December, the early morning temperature was still quite fresh during my first visit to Luang Prabang. The fame of this place rested largely in its vast number of pagodas, all true gems dedicated to Buddhist worship. Magnificent ornaments carved on the walls and the outer doors of the numerous temples tell historic tales about the capital of the ancient Kingdom of a Million Elephants. With mounting excitement I anticipated that this visit to the world heritage site of Lan Chang culture promised to reveal to me a whole string of gems of ever increasing beauty.

Immediately the Wat Mai confirmed this expectation by its originality and richness. A majestic five-tiered roof dominates the lower tiled roofing that covers a peristyle built on the front to protect the modest entrance. Massive pillars, painted gold on a black background, support this doorway, on which are gold bas-reliefs, intricately decorated and depicting the legend of Phravet, one of the last

The pagodas in the hills of Luang Prabang.

incarnations of the living Buddha. This edifice built by King Arunut in 1794, then restored by King Mantaturaj, is home to the venerated statue of the Buddha Phra Bang during three days of the Pimai, the Laotian New Year. Luckily I would have the chance to be fully involved in these festivities, for the house standing in front of this temple, belonged to a warm and generous family, of which I was fortunate enough to be welcomed as a full member.

Sitting on their doorstep, I spent several hours planning the best perspective from which I could faithfully portray this architectural splendour. But before I could start any drawing or painting I needed a chance to have a general look around. This would allow me to satisfy some of my curiosity and confirm the wonderful things I had already heard about this city. It would also allow me time to make decisions on formulating an aesthetic approach and also to arrange in my head a schedule of the work to do.

So, my stroll continued and a few hundred yards further on, I reached a second temple, the Wat Sen. Its construction was started in 1683 and was only finally

The monks gather at Wat Sen before a monthly ceremony in the occasion of the full moon.

revitalized by an important addition in 1957. Carved wood, shrouded in golden lacquer, garnished the inside, where wall frescos depicted several holy places, such as the Burmese Chewedogong Chedi or the Indian Buddha Khaya Chedi. Very different from the previous temple, this one towered up in a more elementary and common configuration. The overhanging roof protecting the doorways to the temple sits on six relatively high columns, topped by a very sharp adorning spire, called in Laotian "Nhot So Fa', stretching the silhouette of the pagoda in an amazingly impressive way. This majesty might explain the presence among the residents of the most senior monk of the Buddhist community of Luang Prabang.

At this time, this greatly respected monk, in line with the discipline of his calling, was eating his only meal of the day with his disciples. Taking advantage of this lull, I sat down for a while on beams piled up in the courtyard. These pieces of wood reminded me that the life of monks is not only a matter of religious duties, but includes building and maintenance tasks. Behind me stood a row of Kutis, little shelters for novices, with space only for a bed and very few belongings. This clearly reflected the Buddha's teachings and overall philosophy, valuing, as it does, meditation and detachment from material possessions.

The first rays of the sun were beginning to bathe the fine adornments on the top of the façade; stirring in me a personal Buddhist-rooted contemplation. Against a blood red background made watery by bad weather, the many interwoven golden arabesques were unveiled with fluidity and clearness under this caressing light. I suppose that I was sinking into the deep pleasure of contemplating this spectacle rather than involving myself in a real meditation. These sweet tempered early hours nearly made me almost forget my need to continue with my explorations.

So, whilst committing these images to memory, I extricated myself from dreaming and went back up the street to the Wat Xieng Thong. Seated at the north eastern end of the town, it is the last but most prominent element of this trilogy of temples. Considered as the greatest gem of the city, it had been built under King Chaiyachetthathiraj, who reigned around 1559-1560, to celebrate the memory of the legendary King Chantapanith. The "Ubosot', the leading building, is rather medium-sized with the characteristic bird wing curved roof slope of Lan Chang architecture.

From the "Nhot So Fa' style spire, once again finely worked, tiled side roofs sweep downwards nearly to the ground, to protect the mural stenciled embellishments of gold on black, which link the two legends of Thao Sisouthone and Thao

Detail of the refined Wat Xieng Thong, considered as the Buddhist gem of Luang Prabang.

Souttasom. The wide courtyard is accessible from three open gates on adjacent streets and gives entry to a group of dwellings, the presence of which helps explain the permanent numbers of inhabitants, joined regularly by tourists in the enclosure of the temple.

Opposite to Wat Xieng Thong, a bigger building shelters a royal funeral carriage and a collection of liturgical objects behind a façade richly carved in a glittering golden hue, which, were the sun to be flashed straight on to it could easily burn the eyes. Just as remarkable, a glass and mica encrusted mosaic, depicting daily life scenes had been done during 1957 on the outdoor walls of the red Chapel, which houses the statue of a reclining Buddha. Dispersed all around are more relics, with the ashes of the worthies who spent their life in the temple, remaining in these "Tats', i.e. lime whitewashed sanctuaries. This collection of works of art, including countless "tree of life' designs applied to the temple's back wall as the symbolic origin of the "Golden Town' monastery, reflects the history of this place which enjoyed the patronage of royal families and officials.

Remarkably, Wat Xieng Thong is preserved in its original form having been spared the otherwise near complete destruction of the town 1887 by Deo Van Tri. He was a bandit of evil repute in Luang Prabang. He had chosen to establish his domain here in order to better organize his systematic plunder of the gilded temples. Unfortunately the Buddhist teachings of his novitiate spent here had obviously been forgotten. Providentially, since then a number of restorations have been made, thereby returning to the inhabitants, and nowadays to the public, a large part of the religious and architectural treasures, which had been either stolen or damaged.

In 1914, a cave of previously unknown major relics was discovered. They are now displayed in the throne room of the Royal Palace. Similarly restored is a masterpiece of Luang Prabang history, which had been first built in1552, by King Visunalat who gave his name to the temple. This Wat Visunalat, which had been originally made exclusively of wood with the outline profile of a boat, was quickly repaired after the town's devastation ended. The same enclosure offers a space

The That Chomsi has been built in 1804 by King Anourouth.

for an amazing Stupa. Its real name is the That Pathum, but has been renamed by the Laotians as Mak Mo, i.e. the Watermelon, reflecting its massive and pot-bellied shape. Looking like a bulky structure of cement, this "water-melon' stands against the surrounding refined religious edifices. Through the courtyard's dividing low wall, is a little porch in the Khmer style, leading to the grounds of a more modestly sized temple, the Wat Aham, where two magnificent Buddha trees rise majestically, protecting a row of Kutis from the sun. A special room is reserved in these dwellings to keep the three hallowed masks, incarnations of the town's ancestors. I was fortunate in that I witnessed the checking and preparation of the masks before the official Pimai ceremony. The man in charge of this task was the owner of a workshop where I happily settled down facing the temple main entrance, painting and chatting for hours with his sister, who had kindly lent me a chair.

In order to finish this general survey, I climbed the 328 or so steps leading to the Phousi Mountain so that I could take in the length and breadth of the town. At the start of the ascent, I stopped to have a look at Wat Pa Houak erected in 1861 by Phraya Srimahanam, under the sovereignty of King Chamtarath. On the front, a woodcarving shows Indra riding the Elephants of Erawan. Inside frescos detailed the miracle of Jampoupati, when the Buddha appeared in his greatest magnificence, in order to humiliate an overly presumptuous prince.

Representations of the Buddha in full dress displaying the earth's kingship badge emanate from this tale, to contrast with the classic features of the Buddha wearing the dress of a monk. From 1945 on, the ministry of religious affairs has gathered several manuscripts, using the monastery as Luang Prabang's library. In a final burst of energy I reached the That Chomsi, established as it was on top of the hill in 1804 by King Anourouth. From this position, 150 meters or so up, the town, literally swallowed by the greenery, looks serene and magnificent. The view fully repaid my efforts. Despite the intense greenery it is possible to catch a glimpse of the Royal Palace, built in 1904 under King Srisawanwong, where the royal family spent their life until the end of the reign of King Srisawangwattana. The palace was finally turned into a museum after the advent of the Lao Popular Democratic Republic regime, in 1975.

By contrast, Wat Choum Khong, so called by King Soukhasem in 1840 because of the melodious sound of its drums, was not visible from Phousi Mountain. I had

Top: The author meeting with neighbours.
Center: By the time the monks, as the citizens, get used of the presence of an artist.
Bottom: The author at work.

to come down, and then follow the main avenue looking for an alley, which weaved its way down between some of the most ancient wooden houses. The largest of these houses has become the World Heritage Museum. This little stroll led me to the courtyard of Wat Choum Khong, from where the frescos of the Phra Vet legend can be visited via a short staircase under the guard of two special statues, the "Chineses Ho from Muong Nong He". The right-hand one holds the "Vajra", the lightning symbolizing male virility, and the left-hand one, holds the Ghanta personifying femininity, both evoking the main Boddhisattvas of Chinese Buddhism.

This long walk only revealed parts of the city and I have not attempted a full record of the temples lining the streets of Luang Prabang. A lifetime of work would not be sufficient to fully record these wonders. So during the eight months out of the two years I was privileged to be there, I merely tried to represent my personal preferences. Initially ink sketches were done on a small drawing pad - this being a discreet way of working that allowed the monks and inhabitants to become used to the presence of an artist.

The sequence in which the paintings were completed closely follows the sequence of my description of the temples. Starting with the Wat Sen, because it seemed to be of the most manageable shape to begin with, the set includes Wat Mai, and Wat Xieng Thong, all done in the classically figurative style. The actual painting activity required me to work at the same time every day in order to catch the decorations and complexities of line that seemed to continually change under the sun's path *(Portrait sun 4-5h). In this way, two paintings were emerging in parallel, one from the gentle morning light, and the other under the warmer afternoon sun. Generally people were keeping me company as I worked, revealing to me through their anecdotes some of the city's secrets.

I was especially blessed whilst painting the interior view of the Wat Xieng Thong as the monks prayed and sang for one hour at dusk. I can still vividly remember the low and monotonous sound of their psalms suddenly heightened by a soprano voice of a very young novice who was often late, having been engrossed outside in a game with friends. Having noticed my presence at the far end of the temple and seeing my watercolor equipment, he appealed to the other monks to come and look at my work. So instead of rushing off quickly after their prayers, the youngest monks surrounded me and begged the monk responsible for the lighting to delay its extinguishing. They chatted animatedly as each one tried to identify his own silhouette or check the accuracy of the details of the nave.

Wat Mai, its intricate ornaments required several studies.

As Thai and Laotian are rather similar languages it was easy for me to understand their chatter, as well as the stories of the many people who talked to me whilst I worked. All this gradually heightened my perceptions, both visual and mental allowing for an increasingly personal interpretation to emerge in the paintings being done. In the picture of the Wat Aham I attempted to emphasize the aura of Buddhism emanating from the legends still told about the two august trees. The leaves of the foreground flew off more in my imagination than in reality as I tried to evoke the legend of the Buddha meditating under their shade. At the same time I worked to retain the uniform simplicity of my work and avoid a composition that would be too surrealistic.

Equally the statues at the entrance of Wat Choum Khong are disproportionate, to emphasize the strength of their symbolic personification, which I felt would not have emerged in a more conventional illustration.

I wanted to build up my work in the reporter's style with the intrinsic assumption that it should be the duty of an artist to find a way to portray the essence of places. Even so I often seemed to be choosing a roundabout way to get closer to what I perceived as certain truths.

Left: Wat Aham under the spell of a magnificent Buddha tree and its legend.

Following double-page: That Chomsi stands some 150 meters over the town as the original center of the town.

ພະທາດພູສີ ຫລວງພະບາງ ລາວ

Executed from the house of my relatives living just in front, the final work about Wat Mai.

A Not So Fa, the adornment dressed on the top of the roof of Wat Xieng Thong with its the smooth curved shape characteristic of The Larnchang architecture

Decoration inside Wat Mai, which was originally the shelter for the holy statue Phra Bang

The six impressive columns confer a wider shape to Wat Sen, quite unusual for the temples in Luang Prabang.

Wat Choum Khong with the "Chinese Ho from Muong Nong He" statues.

That Chomsi by night.

The first of the 328 stairs going on top of Phousi Mountain, an exhausting ascension at the hot season.

Wat Pa Houak adorned with a wood carving of the three head's Elephant of Eravan.

Preceeding double-page: That Pathum familiarly called Mak Mo, meaning watermelon.

Prayers gather every end of afternoon in Wat Xieng Thong to recite in chorus the teaching of the Buddha displayed in Bali language.

ຫຼວງພະບາງ
12/11/41/98.
ລາວ

Traditions and festivals

Buddhists rites, festivals and the rhythm of life

The most imposing civilizations have always left their traces on the stones of buildings and artifacts as a heritage for future discovery. Through these fragments of human history, no matter how eroded, later generations have been able to search and find some sense of their human origins, even when this required patience and persistence.

Compared with the Pyramids, Machu Pichu, or the Temples of Angkor, Ayutthaya and Sukhotai, the architecture of Luang Prabang might appear insignificant. Yet in its case there is the wonderful added dimension of centuries old, continuous and enduring amalgamated practice of Buddhist and Animist cultures. The community of Luang Prabang still resonates with these traditions, which add a specific dimension to enhance the justification of its admission to the ranks of world heritage sites. Jostled by historical and political tumults, the city retained its soul by

Pimai procession with the Queen of the Year to lead the cortege.

standing up to the test of battles between numerous different interests, whilst leaving its cultural roots still deeply anchored in the heart of Laotians. This is evidenced by all pervading day-to-day religious practices.

Before dawn, the gongs resound in the temples, mixing with the cry of the cockerels to signal the monk's and inhabitant's hour of wakening. Under a thread of mist barely pierced by the sun's first rays, the procession of the bronzes leaves the temple in its quest for daily offerings. Several groups of five, ten, thirty or more saffron-robed monks walk along the streets in every district in the "Tak Bak" ceremony.

Kneeling respectfully, by the side of the roads, housewives wear the conventional but iridescent colored silk sarong, doubled at the front into a straight skirt, which falls down to the ankle and is fixed at the waist with a belt of silver. The men folk join their wives, with finely embroidered clear scarves tied across their chests. Set down in silver cups especially appointed for this purpose, the freshly prepared glutinous rice holds its warmth in its small wicker baskets, waiting

Tak Bak: a faithful waiting for the monks going out of every temples to collect alms in the earlier morning.

A fair in a neighbouring village during the Hmong New Year, just few days before the Christian New Year.

to be scooped up into the rounded urns that the monks present while passing by. On feast days, these offerings can be added to with fruit, biscuits or sweets. The giving finished, donors join hands at their foreheads to signal their formal acknowledgments and good wishes to the Buddha's representatives.

The givers accumulate merit, which improves their karma that will guarantee, for themselves and their family, reincarnation of higher status. This wished for state is still far off, although at least this day has started with good intentions. Now the time has come to turn to more everyday matters.

Even so, these more humdrum activities will be interrupted by other events that will reflect more specific types of Laotian celebrations. The receiving of visitors, parental journeys, professional or school successes, births, marriages, funeral services, and other things will be the excuse for a "Bacci". On such occasions neighbours, friends and family members will meet around a magnificent arrangement

Monks on their early morning collection amid a Serene surrounding of old houses and trees.

of flowers, banana leaves plaited and pricked into a cone-shape, all set round with fruits, biscuits and sweets. Some candles illuminate this masterpiece, which will be surmounted by twisted thread fringes, which is crucial to ensure a successful ceremony.

The "Mophon", usually an elder of the community, who has dedicated part of his existence to the traditions and culture, leads what was originally an animist ritual. His status allows him to establish a calendar from which he can select the most propitious day on which to hold a service.

The ritual starts with the elder leading the prayers. The cords of the twisted thread fringes are attached to the wrists of the guests surrounding the Bacci tray. The most honored member of the group will be the first to receive a cord bracelet whilst, as ceremony master, the elder declaims a legend linked to the reason for the occasion and punctuates it with sigh for happiness and success. During a special celebration like a marriage or a birth, the participants may carry on knotting the cords around their wrists in turn, until their forearms are nearly covered. Bacci ceremonials like this take place in a very cordial atmosphere and they always end with a shared meal. By preserving the bracelets for at least three or four days, the celebrants hope that the benefits gained from the ceremony will be maximized.

The culture of an altruistic community is deeply ingrained in the life of Luang Prabang. This never-ending contact of ritual between the citizens of the city represents once again the real treasure of this world heritage site. The modern overlauded cult of individualism has partly eroded this ancient notion of brotherhood. Such daily acts of communion can take on even more significance at the time of a major event, and may well stretch beyond district meetings, as the whole city becomes involved.

The high point of this cultural expression takes place during the festivities of the Pimai when Laotians celebrate the Buddhist New Year in mid April. Several types of ritual take place one after the other during this special week, with preponderance given to those that specifically venerate Buddha and his disciples. The statue of the Phra Bang comes out of its retreat in the Royal Palace and stands for

A Bacci: specific ceremony in Laos, attended that time at my friend's house to welcome family members.

the three days within the Wat Mai enclosure. Whole families come down to put bunches of arranged flowers, candles and incense sticks at the feet of this talisman to show their respect and formulate their own individual prayers. Then, climbing on a dais with a silver beaker, the supplicants pour fragrant water into a wooden bird carved at the tip of a long wooden pipe. At its opposite end is a large ornamental Dragonhead about one meter above the upright Phra Bang. The purified water that streams onto the statue in a cascade of droplets refracts the candles flames in a myriad of gold sparks through the slight veil of smoke rising from the incense sticks. All the inhabitants of Luang Prabang pay tribute in this way, while the monks stand watch in continuous day and night shift.

A sign of the times, a television set is installed for the occasion, and shows the type of films that the novices along with all teenagers enjoy. Some purists regret these changes but I delighted in the ambiance of this evening of mixed religious reverence and entertainment.

Watercolor work is, as the name implies, a simple technique where water is used as the basic ingredient, diluting the pigments before they are applied to the paper. Paradoxically despite the heat wave and drought of the Pimai days before the arrival of the monsoon, there was no shortage of water on the streets. Following the gentle sprinkling of holy water on the monks procession in the city streets, the feast turned into a more buoyant mood as the young Laotian's high spirits lead them to freely and systematically soak anyone passing within reach of their containers. This is way beyond paper's acceptance of watercolor. Add to this watery extravaganza handful of liberally distributed flour, which raining down on my artwork could turn my painting into depictions of falling soot, and you can understand my anxiety to avoid seeing these additives mix with the colors of my pictures. Therefore, I decided not to paint for a few days and to allow myself the pleasure of simply taking part in the festivities with the Laotians and the numerous tourists who abound at this time.

Taking advantage of a sunny spell between the ever-punctual arrival of the monsoon storms, I drew some picturesque and happy things on my sketchpad. From my strategic balcony refuge, I was able hastily to sketch a record of the Pimai procession with its « queen ». She was perched on a model representing the relevant zodiac sign of the Buddhist calendar. To win this annual prized position, local young women have to vie with one another over previous evenings. By parading in their extremely beautiful dresses made of traditional Laotian silk, they are judged on their elegance. Attracted by the ambiance of an open-air party the population attends the presentations, song recitals, dances, and other entertainments.

Joyful pilgrimage crossing the Mekong during the Pimai.

Be it an evening fair, or a morning market with bazaar, children from seven to seventy seven years old can seek and find their own special treat. An exotic fish, a gardening utensil, an old music instrument, or a red balloon, there is something for everyone. In addition, nobody forgets to make a wish when he buys a little cage to free the bird trapped within. These secular attractions alternating with the religious ceremonies pull together all generations, thereby guaranteeing the continuity of these traditions. Everybody meets to climb Mount Phousi, putting down on the Naga's body wads of glutinous rice and handfuls of confectionery, which gradually become a sculpted banister. Whilst their parents are preoccupied with their prayers, the children take the opportunity to escape and cheekily amass of as much as they can manage of this bounty before rejoining their families in the procession down the other side of the hill.

As the Pimai celebrates the arrival of a New Year, the citizens try to invoke the most propitious environment in which to welcome new spirits who may influence their lives over the coming year. To this end houses are cleaned and tidied and relics and religious ornaments are polished. In this environment, the 'Ancestors' of Luang Prabang, Phu Nyeu and Nya Nyeu accompanied by a Lion. leave their retreat in the Wat Aham, and add their contribution to the process. Personified by thick masks decorated with vegetable fibers, these mythical characters are said to have created planet Earth, and then to have planted gourds from which mankind emerged. Chosen for their virtue and hardiness, three young Laotian men adopt the disguises to lead the procession to the Wat Xieng Thong including a stop at the Phra Bang displayed in the courtyard of the Wat Mai. In every temple, they perform holy dances in order to ensure the blessings of the spirits, and to solicit their benign protection.

In the same jubilant mood, the population embarks in hundreds of boats, crossing the Mekong in pilgrimage to the underground cave of Wat Tham where there are a vast number of Buddhas. Armed with paper garlands and flags decorated with the zodiac signs, the ebullient crowd jumps into the water before they have even reached the opposite bank that the drought and the consequent low river level has exposed as a vast expanse of sand. In small groups, the participants first get involved in a contest to shape the most beautiful stupa of damp sand in which they plant their garlands, suddenly transforming this bank into a seeming outcrop of mushrooms. This small pilgrimage done, the afternoon ends in a frolic in the water before everyone re-crosses the river to continue the Pimai celebrations.

Even though I lived in Luang Prabang for eight months, I was unable to see and record all the ceremonies, religious and secular that happen throughout the year. Among those I missed was the race of colored pirogues during October at the end of the monsoon. Every visitor undertaking a journey to Luang Prabang at any time of the year would be unlucky if, over a period of a few days, they did not witness a at least one magical religious ritual.

Full animation in the streets, between entertaining fair and religious deference.

Nearly all citizen of Luang Prabang cross the Mekong to build their sand stupas.

Following double-page: A meticulous composition prepared for "tamboon", a donation routine in the Buddhist practice to acquire a good Karma.

1000
500

A holy shower of flowers falling from frangipanis, from which emanates a memorable fragrance.

Another typical composition prepared for "tamboon", a donation routine for the Buddhist.

Buddha Phra Bang stands for three days at Wat Mai during Pimai and welcomes the respect from the entire community of Luang Prabang.

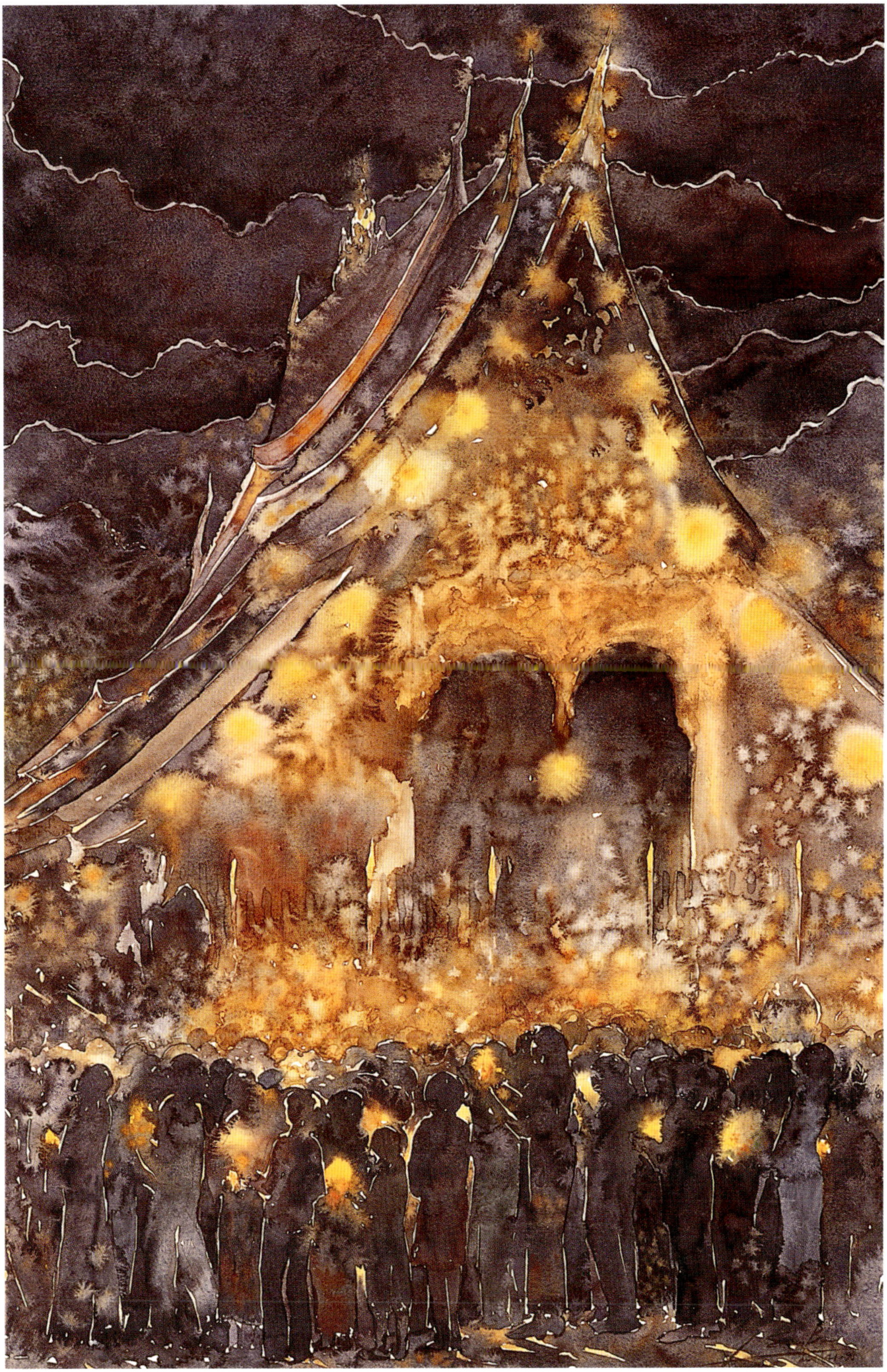

A night ceremony at Wat Xieng Thong.

Preceeding double-page: Pimai procession at Wat Xieng Thong, one of the outstanding occurrence during the New Year celebration in Luang Prabang.

An intensive shower during the week of Pimai is very appreciable as the weather culminates at the hottest time of the year.

Following double-page: Candles and flowers lay down to pay respects at the Buddha Phra Bang.

Preceeding double-page: The queen of the Pimai in front of Wat Mai, during 1998, celebrating the New Year of the pig in the Buddhist calendar.

Previous double-pages: The ancestors of the town: Phu Nyeu, Nya Nyeu and the Lion go out from their retreat once an year for the Pimai celebration.

Sand stupas set up in hundreds on the bank of the Mekong, among the numerous Buddhist rituals of the New Year celebration.

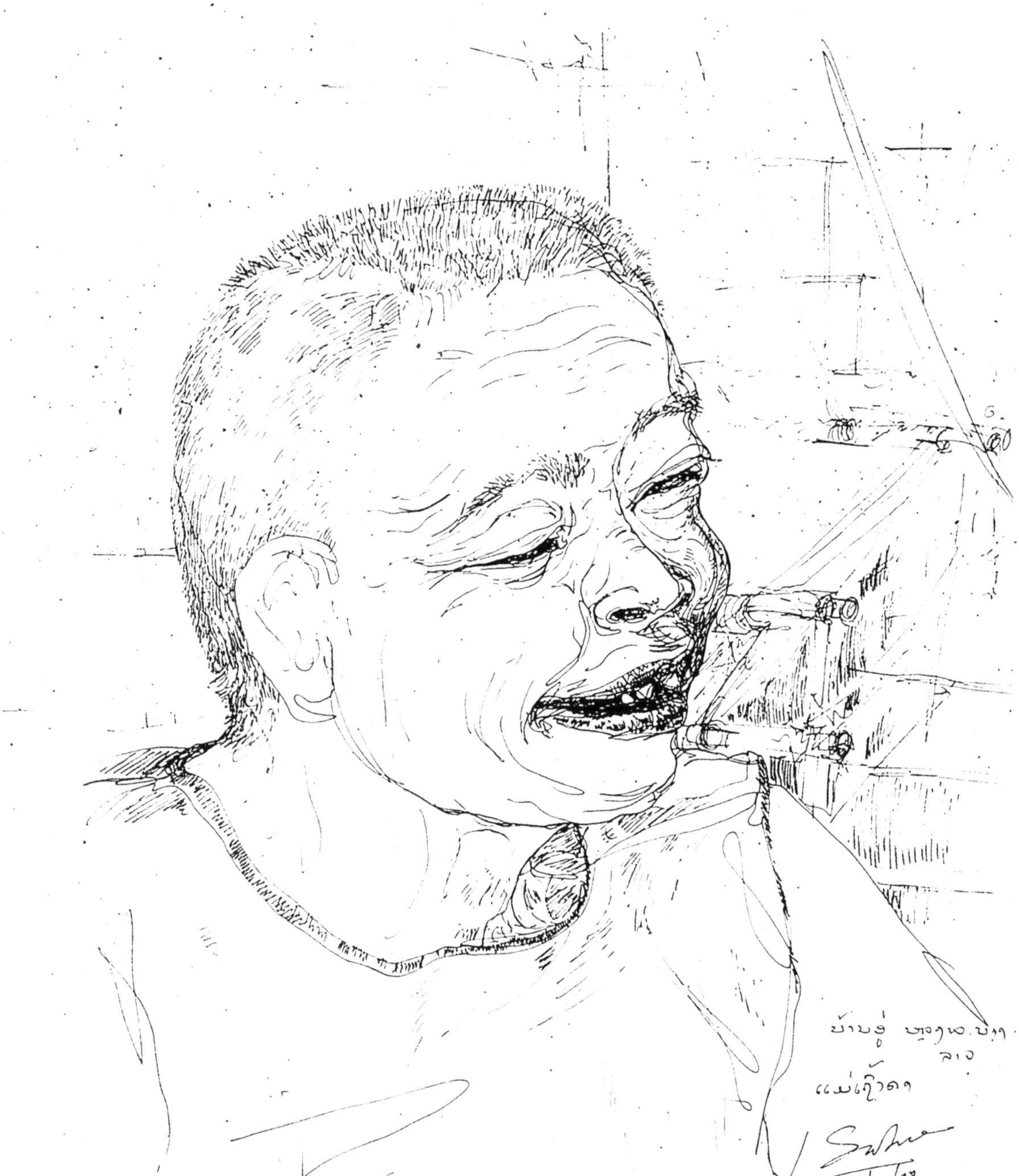

The smile of an old lady chewing too much betel.

A certain way of life

Animated streets, with a natural kindness

Very early one morning, I went out to visit the Santi Chedi temple, accompanied by our friend, Seny, an American photographer who speaks fluent Laotian. His professional assignment this time offered this native of Luang Prabang a return to his roots. We had met by accident and had hit it off straightaway when I was working in the street on a watercolor painting of the house of my Laotians friends, of whom Seny is a relative. When he first saw my pictures he was full of praise for my work. He was particularly enthusiastic about the practice of a medium other than photography being used to record the life and customs of the city of which he was so fond.

A water wheel around Luang Prabang, discovered on the way to Kuangsi falls, very popular with tourist.

At the end of this morning outing together we had hired a tuk-tuk for our return journey. At this time of day the streets around the markets were bustling. Not wanting to miss any element of the unfolding spectacle around us, we watched everything intently, whilst discussing which tableau we would wish to capture for our own commissions. As ever this was a never-ending topic of conversation for us.

Suddenly, Seny drew my attention to the jerky staggering gait of a peddler collapsing under the load of two vegetable baskets balancing over her shoulders. As we stopped at the only red light in Luang Prabang, which controls the traffic on and off the metallic bridge at the south entry to the city, the woman drew level with us. Without a word, Seny jumped from the tuk-tuk and started an animated conversation with her as she jettisoned the baskets at her feet. The noise of the motor obscured the conversation, and unable to read the language of their hands, I asked our driver to wait for a moment whilst I got close enough to hear what was going on. I discovered that Seny was excitedly negotiating the purchase of one complete vegetable basket.

Sketching at a little market makes me a real attraction for the locals.

Street gathering of local women dressed traditionally -ink sketch study.

When the woman began the process of individually wrapping carrots, salads, string beans, and small onions, in plastic bags, he quickly made her understand that he desired not only to buy the contents but the basket too. Disconcerted the brave woman pretended at first not to understand because no one had ever asked to buy her old basket, then suggested that it was not in good condition and therefore not for sale. Besides, she protested, she needed it for her work. Seny kept up his cajoling backed by really tempting prices for the goods. Although still uncertain, once she had confirmed her understanding of the situation and the price offered she reluctantly agreed. Her crestfallen face provoked roars of laughter from our friends and interested passers-by who had stopped to witness this bargaining. Still somewhat confused, the peddler struggled to balance the remaining basket at the tip of her pole. She left with a lighter physical load but with a mind weighed down with questions about this extraordinary encounter with such an odd customer.

Proud of his acquisition Seny gave the basket to me whilst climbing back into the vehicle. He then told me what a wonderful subject his purchase would make for a still life. He also insisted that I paint the vegetables immediately before their freshness had faded, adding that the quicker this was done the quicker his aunt would be able to use them in one of her famous recipes for all our later enjoyment.

I have always enjoyed looking at and cultivating flowers or green plants, so much so that had I not dedicated myself to a career in art I feel I could have made an excellent gardener. My previous studies of vegetation and floral compositions helped considerably in noting the enormous variety of colors, including a vast shades of green, in this still life. So, taking Seny's advice, I painted swiftly seeking to match the freshness of the vegetables with the rapid production of the picture, and happily this watercolor appeared like a breath of fresh air, in welcome contrast to the long hours taken in reproducing the complex details of the religious buildings. This interlude had also shown me a particular tradition, preserved by the conservative nature of the life of Luang Prabang.

The stall holders here still bunch together the vegetables they display for sale with thin strips of bamboo and this custom, practically lost everywhere else in Laos, are still used as a distinctive means of attracting shoppers to their stall. Day after day, the women spend much of their time tying these bunches of vegetables meticulously while waiting for their regular customers. To relieve the monotony of this task, the older stall holders often take out a small tin, which contains an assortment of plants, powder and betel walnut. From this they make a paste which they manage to chew without ceasing their endless chatter. Over time this mixture blackens their teeth, coloring their smile a brownish red that the younger women stallholders find repellent and, nowadays, have abandoned this custom.

A number of women have also fortunately perpetuated, from their Laotian ancestors, the crafts of spinning and weaving of both silk and basketry, an inheritance requiring tremendous patience. It is always disconcerting to see how easily, apparently unconcerned with this task, they make the meticulous precise movements necessary without ever having to interrupt their conversations.

The preparation of the glutinous rice and sweet mash potato pancakes sprinkled with sesame seeds, whilst less skilful, nevertheless requires constant practice and dexterity. The work involved in peeling vast quantities of potatoes, rubbing them together with gently cooked gluey rice, kneading hundreds of pancakes, spreading them on lattices for a day to dry, taking them off one by one, and finally stacking and wrapping them, I think explained the yawns of one elderly woman I

This woman grilling banana is one of the many merchants you can encounter along the streets to take the edge of your hungry.Street merchant grilling banana.

saw busy with this task. These tasty pancakes were nevertheless an ideal mid-afternoon snack. I often benefited from the productivity of these gentle ladies by tasting all kind of fritters, biscuits, grilled bananas, or sweets, all arranged on a simple table under an oversized awning, such as the one in front of my friend's house.

Every morning that I was painting brought enormous pleasure, not just from the work itself but also from my immersion in the activity and life of the streets in which I found myself. We often started the day with a breakfast in the company of Laotians, in a small restaurant serving the customary noodle soup. Seated on small benches around a low table, not really convenient for my husband's long legs, we mused over the white steam that came out of the one and only pot, everlastingly boiling.

It had blackened the timbers and corrugated iron sheets set up as a makeshift shelter in the front of a former colonial house. It seemed symbolic to see the bourgeois character of this home expressing its western builder's ambitions, reduced to the humbleness of an odds and ends eating-house. Its current state, following its return to the native Laotian population, reflected the more fatalistic philosophy of days spent according to the famous "bo pen yang", or "never mind".

Productivity or profitability concerns are not present in the spirit of this micro-society. Here everyone attends to their own needs by providing the bare essentials for their daily life from the natural environment. Luang Prabang activities are shared between handicraft, market gardening, fishing and subsistence small trade. Soon after the monsoon has passed, the floodwaters of the Mekong drop, revealing the newly fertilized banks, which quickly turn into prolific green gardens. At the height of its dryness the Nam Khan carries large amounts of river-weed, which have proliferated in the heat. At its lowest level the bed of the river is

The author checking work in her room at the guest house.

I was use to spend time with this old Hmong lady, even thought I couldn't understand one word of her language.

easily accessible, and children gather this natural harvest with great pleasure. The plants are cleaned, and then dried before being added to various dishes. Or finely chopped and then stir-fried the river-weed becomes a crusty appetizer, much prized by the local population.

The rivers and their fish are inexorably entwined in the life of this place. Fishing skills are passed from fathers to sons, everyone knows how to steer a dugout, how to cast a net and how to place the hoop net in these waters. Yet, current scientific research confirms the preservation of a remarkable eco-balance with a wealth of more than seventy different species of fish present in the river. The people of Luang Prabang, so dependent on it for life sustaining food, would also be unhappy separated from their rivers for other reasons too. They would, for example, miss the pleasure of evening bathing. Indeed many families do not consider it necessary to put bathrooms in their houses since they have such a ready supply of fresh water running permanently at their feet.

In this picturesque setting the Hmong people, too, add their colorful touch. An integral part of the Luang Prabang social fabric they bring their customs and drive to the markets. Every day the Hmong women settle in the town center, publicly displaying their embroidery. They hail the tourists when they go by, attempting tirelessly to sell one of their magnificent pieces of sewing. One older trader systematically called me with her nasal voice. Her friendly smile under mischievous eyes prompted me to spend some time besides her sketching her portrait. She appeared delighted when I gave her copy of the drawing although I must confess, I could not understand a single word uttered by my new found friend. Surrounded by her neighbors, I was flooded quickly with endless requests for similar sketches of themselves, each one with a large smile, attempting to present her best profile Fortunately my husband came to my rescue, taking some photos in less time than I would have required, which we could take back and give out later. Without this happy intervention I would be drawing portraits still.

During my time in Luang Prabang I shared this calm and simple life. I adopted the Laotian habit of making my purchases either early in the morning before beginning work or at the end of the afternoon, allowing relaxation once the paintbrushes were put away. When we returned to our guest-house, we delighted in its domesticity. I preferred to come straight back to my little "chez moi" after a day at work, thereby avoiding the usual tourist search for a restaurant in which to eat. My husband or I prepared our evening meal in the kitchen of our hosts. Then often, during the cold period, we were welcomed to join them in front of their television set, wrapped up in blankets to watch a "Thai soap" of which we had seen the first episodes at home in Bangkok. After his long walks to record the life of the city, my husband also appreciated the return to this homely sanctuary, which allowed us to have a quiet meal together whilst exchanging the discoveries and feels of the day. With his portable darkroom he processed his latest black and white pictures and sought my opinion of them.

In turn, he commented on my current painting. Despite watercolor and black and white photography being such different media, these reciprocal critical evaluations were really inspiring, sometimes helping us see the complementary nature of our work. We leave every one to imagine the happiness that we encountered and shared while in the heart of this city, practicing our professional passions while remaining in contact with these people and their life of simplicity and serenity.

Silk spinners are common in the surrounding village.

The house of my family of adoption in Luang Prabang, nicely shadowed and warmly convivial.

Following pages: Women chatting on a local election day:

Above: A big acquisition: a full basket of vegetables, with one of the alternative use above, which is not only for cooking.

Following double-page: On the bare ground, sellers display their merchandise in a buoyant atmosphere.

A peddler, who must have been relieved of her burden afterwards.

During my sojourns in Luang Prabang I was a regular in this market, which was not only a store of food but was also a source of inspiration.

Bunches of vegetables: traditional packaging in Luang Prabang.

Betel nuts set to make up this unique dark red smile on the face of old women.

Handicraft and baskets shop among the secular activities lining the streets of Luang Prabang.

A little fabric of dried pancakes, ideal for a mid afternoon snack.

1926

Preceeding double-page: Set up in front of the remains of a colonial house, a small restaurant prepares the noodle soup, one of the favorite breakfast for the locals.

The Hmong handicrafts stand holders, one hand on their embroidery, one hand to call the tourists passing by.

1938

Charm of an ancient city

A green shelter for an architectural treasure

The magnificent gems of Architecture found in Luang Prabang deserve a setting so sensitive that it magnifies their purity and brilliance. Fortuitously the natural envelope of trees cocooning the pagodas acts as in a green iridescent bower, wrapping the temples and the traditional house clusters in a tranquil harmony. Here, no concrete bulk would dare to show its ugly silhouette over the curved roofs, which slip between the tips of the Not So Fa and the tops of the coconut trees.

After the devastation at the end of the nineteenth century (by Yunnanese invaders), cement and bricks quite often replaced the wood of the traditional Laotian cottages that had become so ramshackle. However these replacement buildings never rose up too high and their pastel hues reflected either the sunset, the azure of the sky or the sandiness of the Mekong's banks. When muddy mildew grew like engravings on the walls, or tattoos of rust appeared on the sheet metal,

The last workshop of Ramayana masks maker in the city..

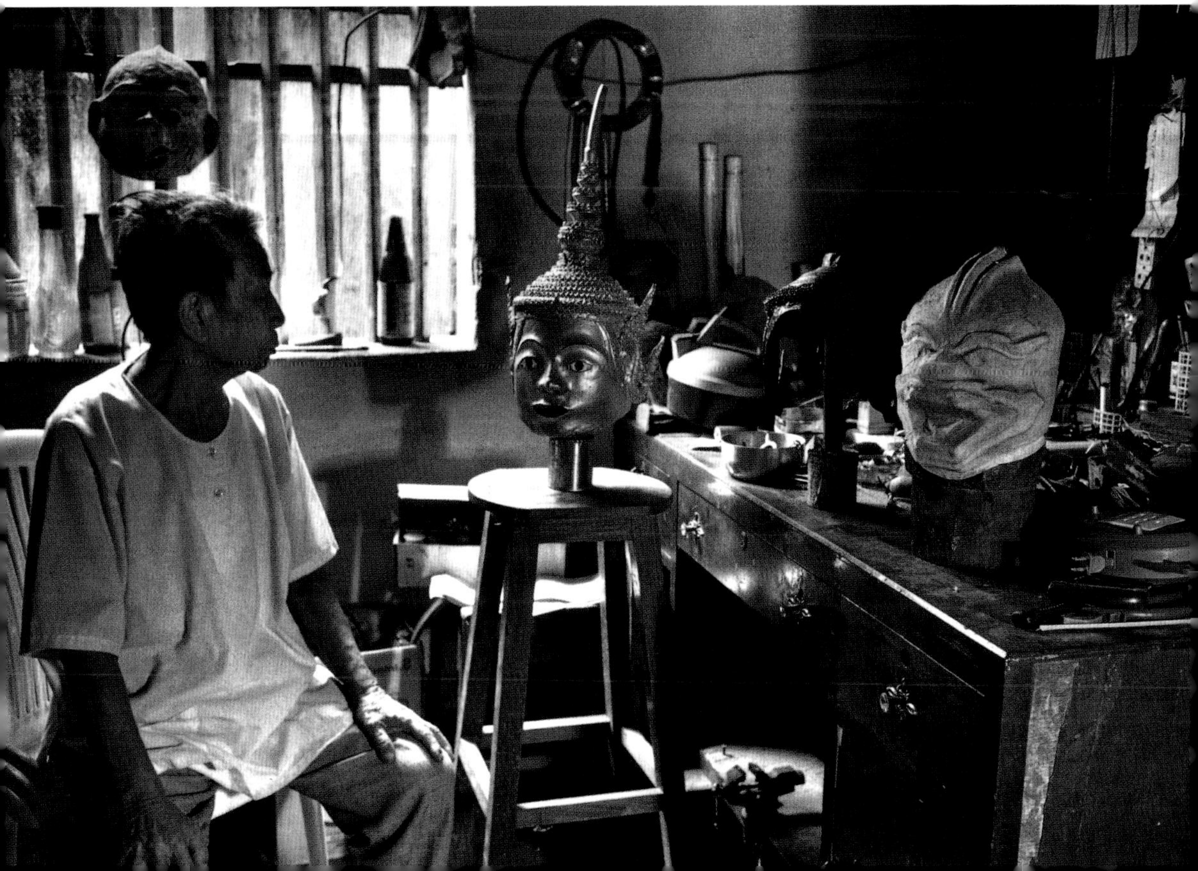

used as emergency roofs, were joined by the streaming rain of the monsoon, these last time-worn touches emphasized the ancient and sacred aspect of the city.

Among the remains that UNESCO discovered and restored was a wooden house of pure Laotian tradition. Fittingly this became a museum detailing the architectural evolution of Luang Prabang. Among a mass of information it is possible to learn, for instance, that the height of pillars supporting the main body of these dwellings was in direct relation to the social status of the owner. From the main

street the French settlers extended the street's geometric layout, adding when necessary small bridges to ensure the continuity of their plans designed to provide for easy navigation and traffic flow in this "village".

During the first half of the twentieth century, endeavoring to retain some Laotian style in the construction of houses of a bourgeois form, western architects incorporated in their designs a few elements copied from other Indo-Chinese colonies. The date stones still remain on the gables of these colonial buildings for which balconies, terraces and ventilation systems were incorporated to try to mitigate the effects of life in a tropical climate. Inspired by Chinese or Vietnamese styles decorative patterns are reproduced on many front walls. I was able to paint one such decoration on a restaurant whilst I was settled on the low surrounding wall of the provincial information center and culture situated directly opposite.

I only had to cross the street to take a break and to sip a fruit cocktail on this restaurant terrace in the company of its owner. This erudite old man proved to be a wonderful source of historical memory and detail. He generously opened up his shop at the back of his house where some strange masks, hanging on frames, were waiting to be brought to life. It became apparent that this man of Luang Prabang is the last creator of props for the Phalak Phalam, the traditional Laotian theatre, and the equivalent of the Thai Ramayana traditional theatre. Sadly, only one of his sons had shown any interest in learning the secrets of this art. Working this day he was painting small decorative mouldings of ash blended with plant resin applied to a mask which was a mixture of papier-mâché, cloth and crushed pieces of Balsa wood.

With the advent of television and new technological entertainment, the interest in this type of theatre has considerably diminished, especially with the young. This gives rise to the fear that this particular profession may disappear without the protection it so desperately needs as a Luang Prabang legacy. --If requested, many tales could seep out of the chinks in the walls or fly out through the gaps in the roofs of these shacks. For example, this proud villa could reveal endless stories about its inhabitants' moods from the top of its colonnades. It was home to the last princess of the royal lineage, who now lives her life like any ordinary citizen, far away from the respect and pomp that her rank would previously have commanded. On the other side of the main street, the small police station has been practically abandoned since the world heritage declaration in 1998. Previously all visitors passing by had to report their arrival and leave their details there

A sketch of the Kuangsi falls, to remind that Luang Prabang is surrounded by greenery.

as required by the authorities. Similarly, the kuti within the enclosure of Wat Mahatat retains numerous records of past lives in its interior according to the old monk who currently lives there. He told me that the entire woodwork of the interior and the big library had been rearranged as originally set out by a prince of the royal family who completed his novitiate in the pagoda.

Often the older people I met were able to tell me stories about the past lives of this place. Among them was a little old white-haired woman, sunk in a squat armchair guarding the entrance to a workshop with its pretty flower filled balcony that had attracted my attention. Seated on a high step on the opposite side of the street, painting this façade, I wondered if this grandmother had witnessed the construction her residence or if indeed she had been born there. Rooted in her seat, she spent her days detachedly watching the activities around her. She only became animated when she had to call out to one of her granddaughters when a tourist asked about renting a bicycle from the family shop. A neighbour told me that she felt that in this manner this grandmother seemed to be awaiting her death. She hardly ever moved out of her place only going in to lie down at dusk. So what a great surprise I got one morning when I saw her moving towards

The picturesque attitude of a woman mending the fishing net for her husband.

An old admirer, who exceptionally crossed the road to come and see what I was painting; what a surprise when she realized that it was her house.

me. The years weighed down this old woman, who could no longer straighten up, but on this second day of my painting her, curiosity had got the better of her.

She obviously longed to know what I was doing in her neighbourhood with my large drawing pad. Carefully she had glanced right and left before slowly crossing the street and, still doubled up, she had come to stand discreetly behind me. Intent on not putting off her approach by always staring at my sheet of paper, I pretended to work, concentrating intently in case I intimidated her. Acutely aware of her presence over my shoulder, I gradually turned toward her, catching her gentle smile. As she apparently couldn't at first sort out what I was attempting to record I began to point out some details of my watercolor. Her eyes sparkled with recognition as she began to make out elements of her house. On the days that followed she came back to keep me company and talk to me as I completed my painting. When the time came to color in the silhouette of her seated in the armchair, I jokingly asked her whether she might not prefer to be recorded wearing a more colorful blouse than her usual grey or beige. My suggestion of pink or spring green or red instantly provoked much hilarity. Seeing the elfin face of this old woman near the end of her life explode into such joy is a memory I shall always treasure. It made me reflect on the use of my art more than many serious or informed critiques might. I feel it is sometimes really helpful and thought provoking for a practicing artist to ignore for the moment the professional critics, and be directly aware of the appreciation of one person's spontaneous and heart felt response.

Criticism, from experts as well as from laymen, should always be considered, even though it's not a requirement to take the comments to heart. In some cases an artist can disappoint their public, as was the case when I attempted a painting of the front of a souvenir shop with blue tinted panelling. Whereas I was striving to reproduce as accurately as possible the decorative mouldings of the house's balcony, the owner asked me to paint in a missing piece of the design as if it were really present in one corner. I tried to explain to her that, I was currently working at producing the most faithful rendition possible and that this broken fragment emphasized her home's true ancient character. Her exasperated expression showed her total disagreement with my views. No doubt her pride lead her to wish to present her home in the best possible light and so a representation of it in perfect condition was important. This would ensure that any public member thereafter who saw my picture could not make judgments about her ability to maintain her dwelling properly in perfect taste. Maybe this woman just wished that a magic brushstroke could restore her shop or could have incited the spirits to rebuild the house with modern materials. I am always amused by the contrast between the owners and inhabitants of these antique dwellings and their attraction to flashy modernism with all its gadgets, and the visitors who arrive from countries swamped with these things who seem to long to rediscover and to preserve the authenticity of the older styles of architecture and living.

Since the city was made a part of World Heritage, contact with the western world is intensifying quickly with the spread of the tourism. Let's hope that the siren voices of money making won't be the defining influence on young Laotians and that they will be able to listen the sensible advice of their elders in order to preserve their treasure intact. Obviously the improvement of material and sanitary conditions in Luang Prabang is a positive step forward for the population. However it is to be wished that the side effects of the financial manna provided by tourism does not destroy the core of this heritage that leans equally on a culture, an art of living, and the stones and wood of its architecture.

Luang Prabang should be considered as a test of a will to preserve the culture and the value of community life. As everywhere this style of life is under constant threat and I believe we must all become aware of the pressing need to preserve this authentic, ancient way of life. Otherwise it will seem as if the very stones of

Up to Tam ting cave to pay respects to a thousand or so Buddha's relics.

Luang Prabang have a greater right to claim they have souls than those who visit this unique place.

This little bridge under the shade of coconut's trees was built to ensure the continuity of the streets in the plans from French architects.

Following double-page: An edge of bougainvilleas adorning the front of a typical house.

A greenery of banana's trees is refreshing the street going down to the newly restored world heritage museum.

A balcony decked out with flowers as usual in many houses of the main street of Luang Prabang

The traditional silk in the front of a shop, is not only for a tourist purpose. The women are still wearing the beautiful silk sarong.

The marks of the monsoon on habitations.

A good shelter from the scorching sun to enjoy a local meal. Admittedly, this house must have been the property of someone of note, referring to the noticeable height of its sustaining pillars.

Above: The villa of the princess, the last descendant of the royal family.

1940

1940

A monk kuti at Wat Mahatam, which has been a shelter for a prince of the royal family during his novitiate.

The blue house with a little broken adornment on the balcony, which the owner wanted me to restore in the painting.

The house of the last Ramayana masks maker, adorned with a Vietnamese style rosace.

Following double-page: The shop of my old admirer, where tourist can rent a bicycle to go easily around as Luang Prabang is mainly flat and not very sprawling.

1938

The date of construction appears on the façade of an old colonial house let by the French.

A Last Thought About Luang Prabang

At nightfall the That Chomsi perched right on top of the Phousi Mountain sparkles brilliantly under its floodlights, like many of the world's other large monuments. Before the advent of electricity the shrine was flooded only by moonlight, bouncing off its gold arrow to end its race in the depths of the Mekong. Such lights seem to convert the river into a magical stream whose mystical power emanates throughout its meandering path.

Its undulations are said to evoke the benevolence of Naga a seven headed, protective snake, who sheltered the meditating Lord Buddha from the storm. Sceptics will surely smile whilst listening to these legends. But that would discount the attachment and devotion to these allegorical tales which demand respect when the harmony of Luang Prabang is observed. The city seems indeed to breathe under a protective soul. The monks, who maintain an unbroken record as historical custodians of these traditions, resolutely follow the lunar sequences and get together in one of the principal temples at each full quarter moon to pledge their obedience to the teaching of Buddha. Shaved heads and cut fingernails are the external marks of purity necessary to carry through the successful ceremonies.

The frangipani flowers circling in this last triptych, (next page) are for me the final component of such rituals. Mixed with water, they are used at many ceremonies, such as the showering of the relics of the Buddha and his representatives at the New Year's days religious celebrations. The heady perfume they give off in the high season is engraved in my memory, dominating by far the fainter recollection of the acrid smell of the smoke spread by wood fires lit to prepare evening meals. This smoke makes the fog of the river even more impenetrable as if to preserve the intimacy of the city and its legendary guards, the Phra Bang standing at the Great Palace and the Naga resting in the bed of the Mekong river.

The Phousi Mountain and the silver plated Mekong, covered by a cloud of frangipani flowers glistening under the moonlight, is the lasting image that I will keep of Luang Prabang, I had walked its streets, by ways and alleys and painted its splendors over several months. Finally my commitment to a realistic representative style of painting had to be put to one side just for once. A faithful rendition of the wonders of Luang Prabang could not express how this place had entered my heart and soul.

So I chose the elements and composition of this triptych to embody my inner-most enchantment with this special place. I hope too that should you now be pulled by a desire to see it for yourself you will visit it with your heart open to the magic spell it cast on me.

Artist's Profile

Education

Born in 1959, at Prachinburi, Thailand
1976-1978: Thaivichitsilp Art College, Bangkok, Thailand.
1979-1981: Poh Chang College of Arts and Crafts, Bangkok, Thailand.

Exhibitions

1978: lst Vane Croup Exhibition. Rajburi, Thailand
1981; Poh Chang College Art Exhibition, Bangkok, Thailand
1984; SiIpa Bhirasri Arts Festival, Bangkok, Thailand
1985; Exhibition, 25th Anniversary of Goethe Institute, Bangkok, Thailand
1986; 1st International Women in Art Exhibition, Bangkok, Thailand
1987; Exhibition of Aesthetics in Honour of The King. Bangkok, Thailand
1988; Solo Exhibition, Ostbirk, Denmark
1989; Solo Exhibition, Kvindegalleriet, Aarhus, Denmark
1990; Exhibition, Montien Hotel, Bangkok, Thailand
1991; Thai-Japanese Women Paintings, Bangkok, Thailand
1992; 2nd International Women in Art Exhibition, Bangkok, Thailand
1992; Asian Young Artists' Exhibition, Tokyo, Japan
1993; Solo Exhibition, Royal Park Travelodge Resort, Phuket, Thailand
1993-1994; The Art of Swing Exhibitions l and II, Bangkok, Thailand
1994; Solo Opening Showcase, New Art Gallery. -Phnom Penh, Cambodia
1995; Watercolour Festival, Montien Hotel, Bangkok, Thailand
1995; Exhibition: An Artist at Angkor
-May: The Royal Cambodian Embassy. Bangkok, Thailand
-September: The Imperial Queen's Park Hotel, Bangkok, Thailand
-October: Akko Collectors' House, Bangkok, Thailand
1995; Thaise-Vlaansevriendenkring Exhibition, Kookelaere, Belgium
1995-1996; 31st and 32nd Asia Modem Art Exhibitions, Japan
1997 to 2002; Annual Red Cross Exhibition, Montien Hotel, Bangkok, Thailand
1993; Solo Exhibition: Amazing blossoms, Siam City Hotel, Thailand
1993; Solo Exhibition: An artist in Luang Prabang, Rajanakarn Building, Bangkok, Thailand
1999; Solo Exhibition: An artist in Luang Prabang, Royal Meridien Phuket Yacht Club, Thailand
2000; Exhibition: Au Coeur de l'hotel, Royal Meridien Phuket Yacht Club, Thailand
2000; Exhibition: Where have all the flowers gone, Akko Gallery, Bangkok. Thailand
2001; Regards Croisés, Boathouse Gallery, Phuket, Thailand
2002; Exhibition: International women day, Satihan Thamasathan, Bangkok, Thailand
2003; Trace of Faith, Duo exhibition, Montien Hotel, Bangkok, Thailand
2004; September: An Evening With Thai Artists, Royal Thai Embassy , New York, USA
2004; October: An Evening With Thai Artists, Royal Thai Embassy, Washington DC, USA
2005; November to 2006 February: Luang Prabang Scents, Maison Seng Tiane Phanith, Luang Prabang, Laos

2007; November: "Letter from Hanoi", Viet Art Center, Hanoi, Vietnam
2008; May: Collective exhibition "Asia Art Link" The National Museum of Hanoi, Vietnam
2008; July: "Letter from Hanoi", Akko Gallery, Sukhumvit Bangkok, Thailand
2008; September: Collective exhibition "Enchanting Nonthaburi", Thailand
2008; November: Collective exhibition Vane Group 30 Th anniversary, Jamjuree Gallery, Bangkok, Thailand
2009; April:Collective exhibition Black Market, Bangkok Art Center Museum, Thailand
2010; August: Collective exhibition Akko Gallery 20th Anniversary, Bangkok Art Center Museum, Thailand
2011; September: Collective exhibition Vane Group, Jamjuree Gallery, Bangkok, Thailand
2012; March to May: Not Just Beautiful - The New Nature Series, Akko Gallery, Sukhumvit Bangkok, Thailand
2012; June: "Les chemins de Saint Jacques de Compostelle", Roumengoux, Ariège, France
2013; December: Journey with a paint brush, Jamjuree Gallery, Bangkok, Thailand
2014; January: Red Cross Exhibition, Queen Sirikit Art Museum, Bangkok, Thailand

Somboon Phuangdorkmai at her study in Bangkok

Acknowledgements

We wish to give our best thanks the following organisations and peoples, without whom this project won't have taken this shape, in particular for the first edition of the book:

The *Thai Lao Association* and it's President *Khun Arsa Sarasin* for supporting the project

The *Lao Thai Foundation.*

The *President of the Rajanakarn Foundation* for opening it's doors to the first public exhibition of many of the images in this book.

Khun Pisanu Chanvitan who initiate this project.

Susan Atkinson for her insightful rewriting of the book.

Roland Neveu for the reproduction of my watercolour and ink prints and the realisation of this book.

My husband *André Lurde* for his unconditional support and presence all along.

The inhabitants of Luang Prabang for their warm welcome and gentle acquiesence of my work in the field.

Our sponsors and art lovers who supported the work of Somboon.

Published in Bangkok - Thailand
by Asia Horizons Books Co., Ltd

This edition 11/2014 (First published: 2004)

Artwork © by Somboon Phuangdorkmai and photography by André Lurde
Text and captions edited by Susan Atkinson

The Luang Prabang Watercolours book is produced by Asia Horizons Books Co., Ltd.

Design & layout by Asia Horizons Books Co.,Ltd.
Printed in Bangkok by Amarin Printing.

Enquiries about distribution and sale should be directed to the following email:
info@asiahorizons.com

ISBN 9786167277110

www.asiahorizons.com